Big Machines At Work

Cherry Pickers

By Hal Rogers

The Child's World® Inc. ◆ Eden Prairie, Minnesota

Published by The Child's World®, Inc.
7081 W. 192 Ave.
Eden Prairie, MN 55346

Design and Production:
The Creative Spark, San Juan Capistrano, CA

Photos: © 1998 David M. Budd Photography

Library of Congress Cataloging-in-Publication Data

Rogers, Hal.
        Cherry pickers / by Hal Rogers.
            p. cm.
        Summary: Describes the parts of a cherry picker, how it operates,
and the work it does.
        ISBN 1-56766-650-7 (lib. reinforced : alk. paper)
        1. Cherry pickers (Machines) Juvenile literature. [1. Cherry
pickers (Machines)] I. Title.
    TJ1363R.58 1999
    629.225—dc21   99-26591
                                                                       CIP

Contents

On the Job

On the job, cherry pickers lift workers high above the ground. Some things are too high to reach with a ladder.

A cherry picker has a long arm called a **boom.** The workers can fold up the boom when they drive from place to place.

There is a **bucket** on the end of the

boom. Workers stand in the bucket.

The boom raises the bucket high up

in the air. It moves quickly.

Now the workers can reach the **power lines.** Power lines carry **electricity.**

The worker **drills** a hole into a pole. He must be very careful. The power lines are dangerous. He wears special gloves to protect himself.

Cherry pickers have an **outrigger.**

It keeps the machine from tipping over.

Climb Aboard!

Would you like to see where the driver sits?

A cherry picker's driver is called an **operator.**

Driving the cherry picker is a lot like driving

a regular truck. Workers move the boom and

the bucket with **controls.** They are on the

outside of the truck.

19

Up Close

The controls

1. The bucket controls

2. The boom controls

The outside

1. The bucket

2. The boom

3. The outrigger

Glossary

boom (BOOM)
The boom is the long arm on a cherry picker. It moves the bucket up and down.

bucket (BUH-kit)
A bucket is the cup attached to the end of a boom on a cherry picker. Workers can stand in the bucket to reach something high.

controls (kun-TROLZ)
Controls are tools used to help make something work. The controls for a cherry picker are on the outside of the truck.

drills (DRILZ)
If a worker drills something, he or she makes a hole in it. Workers sometimes drill holes into poles.

electricity (ee-lek-TRI-si-tee)
Electricity is energy that creates power. Things such as lamps, televisions, and computers all run on electricity.

operator (OPP-er-ay-ter)
The operator is the person who drives the cherry picker. He or she takes it to where the workers need it.

outrigger (OWT-rig-er)
The outrigger keeps the cherry picker from tipping over.

power lines (POW-ur LYNZ)
Power lines are the wires that carry electricity. Power lines are strung between tall poles.